GOLF...
The Cruellest of Games

by

CHEEVER HARDWICK

THE CHOIR PRESS

ISBN 978-1-910864-99-9

First published in the United Kingdom in 2017 by
The Choir Press

Dedication

This Hopefully Amusing Tome Is Dedicated To
My Wife, Susie, And To My Son, Charles
For Their Love And For
Their Constant Tolerance Of My
Somewhat Idiosyncratic Behaviour And Views.

'Man who hit balls with stick will always live in pain.'

– Chinese Proverb

Jimmy Tarbuck, O.B.E.

Foreword
by Jimmy Tarbuck O.B.E.

GOLF – or as we know it - the Scottish Torture – is a game, and games are meant to be fun.

Fun indeed! I've been obsessed with the game for over fifty years – playing it, reading about it and talking about it.

Cheever Hardwick has his own thoughts and theories on golf, some most unusual, but all very interesting. So sit back and enjoy the read with no gimmies or provisionals.

From Coombe Hill, or Pinheiros Altos and San Lorenzo in the Algarve, all nice places to play and all with superb terraces where we can have a drink and discuss yet another magic round . . .

Cheever and I can be found in my own golfing nirvana on the Algarve . . . so do stop by for a drink with the words "Hello Boys . . . did you play well and what are you having?"

Cheers

Jimmy Tarbuck (Golf Nut)

Brian Evans, PGA Professional. Director of Golf – Quinta do Lago.

Introduction

"I promise you a very funny, sometimes irreverent, but always refreshing overview of the great game of golf, written by a good friend. Also as a professional who has taught him, I know he has experienced the frustration of this game we all love ... actually more than most! Knowing his game as I do, I have to admire how he has kept his cynicism to a minimum, especially towards teaching professionals!"

Brian Evans, PGA Professional
Director of Golf – Quinta do Lago

Contents

Hitting a ball with a stick while following behind some wet sheep . . .

Prologue: The Past

Golf is a form of self-inflicted irritation invented in the dim and murky past by Scottish shepherds in skirts trying desperately to take their minds off the howling winds and freezing rain. Wandering aimlessly behind grazing sheep while wrapped in wet, smelly wool as protection from the elements was the breeding ground of the massive industry which now spans the globe.

As its popularity increased from one shepherd to five or six, whisky was discovered to lessen the agonies of chasing a small ball through bog-ridden pasturelands in foul conditions. It also helped them to ignore taunts from their peers and shrill remonstrations from their wives. Hitting a ball with a stick while following behind soggy and odoriferous sheep in a freezing gale was a definite improvement over spending the day in a smoke-filled hut with a burly wife and a litter of screaming children.

Life in the Scottish Moors had little purpose other than sheer survival. Golf added a new dimension to a less than magical existence. Using a shepherd's crook to hit a hand-wrapped ball made of wet twine vastly increased the pleasure of herding sheep, and it also introduced the normally rather taciturn Scots to camaraderie and the art of conversation . . . albeit with limited success.

Competition began to rear its ugly head with the creation of a goal which would be the measure of one's ability – how few times would one have to hit the ball to reach the top of that hillock in the distance? Then the 'top' of the hillock needed to be defined and a stick was stuck in the ground with a tattered cloth tied to it so it could be seen through the rain and fog. Starting to sound familiar?

The gentle tome that follows this perhaps slightly inaccurate historical introduction to golf will guide the reader through the various stages of taking up and playing the dreaded game ... the sheer physical hell of trying to make your body move in totally counter-intuitive ways to produce illogical results, dress codes demanded in various situations, the theory and the reality 'Golf Clubs', and some of the social ramifications of the game. This is not a sport to be approached by the unwary. Many practitioners of the game are quite sure that golf was invented by Charon, the boatman who carries lost souls across the River Styx to the gates of the Underworld ... mainly because golf can often make Hell look appealing.

Golf was invented by Charon, the boatman who carries lost souls across the River Styx . . .

CHAPTER ONE

What is a Golf Course?

The term 'Golf Course' can be applied to any piece of landscape which has been altered, usually at vast expense, to make hitting the ball up to and into a hole in the ground as difficult as possible. Golf course architects are now employed at roughly the same cost as an aeronautical engineer in charge of designing a stealth bomber. Various types of grasses, trees, sand, etc., are used to create the desired effects and to increase costs as much as possible. These costs are then tripled and passed on to the player in the form of 'Green Fees' which the player must hand over for the privilege of playing.

However, in an effort to simplify things as much as possible, note that there are two basic types of golf course: Parkland and Links. Parkland courses give the impression of being leafy, rather soft landscapes and are usually set in rolling, wooded countryside. However, once the golfer stands on the first tee he realises that every tree, bush and shrub is an obstacle, and the fairways are liberally sprinkled with sand traps, also referred to as 'bunkers'. When your ball lands in one of these, it can take an eternity of flailing to extract it, much to the amusement of one's playing companions.

The usual parkland course wanders about through the woods, providing soothing views as your ball bounces off trees and hurtles into adder-filled bushes. The smooth bits of ground that can be seen in the middle of the long grass, bushes, trees and sand traps are known as 'fairways', but one will have little experience with them until much later. Years of practice and prodigious amounts of the folding stuff are required before there are more than very occasional dealings with fairways.

The areas at the end of the fairways are surrounded by bunkers and the smooth, grassy bits in the middle called 'greens' are designed to produce a line to the hole that can be determined only by truly expert players or by using witchcraft. Various greens exist where the player putts the ball in a direction which has no relationship to the location of the hole. The ball wanders, turns back on itself and perhaps ends near the objective. Professional golfers have been known to whimper, scream and roll about on the ground as they watch their balls progress. Most embarrassing.

The other basic variety of golf course is 'Links'. These were the original golf courses, the majority being set near the seaside in Scotland. Links golf is a totally different sport. The player uses the same implements, but that is where the similarity ends.

Whereas parkland settings require complex sprinkling systems, fluffy white sand in the bunkers and greens like compressed velvet, the links course is a slightly modified track of sand dunes, wild knee-deep grasses, holes, mounds, and bunkers which are incredibly deep with vertical walls. The unfortunate player can disappear into one of these hellish pits for quite a long time, his presence signalled by sprays of wet, clumpy sand flying in the air and streams of extremely inventive profanity. It is often required to play backwards or at least sideways to the desired line of ball flight just to get out of them.

Links fairways are also another matter entirely. Whereas the fairways on a parkland course are nurtured like a small child to achieve a springy, soft texture which elevates the ball nicely on a moist bed of fluffy grass, the fairways on links courses can be likened to the 'buzz-cut' seen on SAS troops in cheap films; they are mown as tight to the hard ground as possible. And the ground underneath this nearly total lack of grass is as hard as steel. As links courses are set near the seaside in andy loam, drainage is instantaneous. No soft, moist ground in sight.

The unfortunate player can disappear into one of these hellish pits for quite a long time.

This, of course, makes enormous sense as most links courses are in places that exist under constant attack from wind, rain, sun, hail, sleet and anything else that Mother Nature has in her quiver. Those who practice the arcane art of golf on links courses do so at their own risk. At least four totally distinct climates are normally experienced in one round. This requires a degree of sartorial preparedness normally needed for a holiday starting in the Bahamas and ending at the South Pole.

Those who aspire to the game must also be aware that all golf courses are subject to their own rules. Some are common to almost all courses, as with having out of bounds markers, tee areas which must be used, etc. However, nearly every golf course, be it public or private, will have its own customs and characteristics. For example, various golf courses, especially in the United Kingdom, are by tradition and deed covered in livestock and one must play through herds of grazing animals and hit the ball out of whatever their digestive systems might have left behind without any free 'lifts'. Others allow dogs to accompany the players, which adds enormously to the atmosphere of the game. There is nothing like playing behind a four-ball with seven unruly Labradors and a yapping poodle.

Therefore the novice should never assume that golf is played in surroundings which are in any way consistent. Every golf course presents its own unique set of obstacles. Simply hitting the ball is in itself an enormous challenge, which is then multiplied tenfold by the variety of courses. Also, the same golf hole on the same course can be played five hundred times and it will never play the same way twice. Add in the variety of possible climatic conditions, as well as the characters of one's playing companions, and you have a game which will never be dull or predictable.

All of these variables are what make up a Golf Course, and also what make a golf course the most rewarding and frustrating sporting environment on the planet.

CHAPTER TWO

The Purchase
of
Basic Equipment

The best way to learn to ride a horse properly is with a minimum of equipment ... bareback, without even a saddle. In a similar vein, the best way to learn to hit a golf ball is also to eliminate confusing equipment and choices ... start with a minimal mixture of used clubs. A putter, a couple of irons, a pitching wedge and a driver will be sufficient. There is nothing worse than someone, 'with all the gear and no idea.'

However nice a thought this might be, most novices will spend a large mound of money on an expensive golf bag, a full set of woods and irons, a ridiculous looking putter and all the rest. Then add in a trolley, balls, tees, an umbrella, and, a bale of the latest appalling clothing in colours designed to frighten horses. This is not an inexpensive sport. Lady golfers, on the whole, are more fashion conscious than their male counterparts and this will be reflected in golf outfits having to match, skirt length being a key consideration, and trousers that must show off the waggling backside to great effect when the ball is being addressed.

However, in today's quite unpredictable world, skirt length might be a consideration for men as well. Indeed, one never knows what might show up on a first tee these days. Transgenderism has given rise to cases of deep-voiced and oddly-attired individuals who could happily play international rugby appearing on the ladies tees and hitting the ball 300 yards. Modern surgery combined with political correctness gone mad can, on occasion, provide some interesting situations.

An expensive golf bag, a full set of woods and irons, a ridiculous looking putter and all the rest.

The key to avoiding an absurd waste of money is to find a professional instructor or club fitter to help advise on what to buy. There is a truly endless variety of clubs, shafts, grips, etc., all of which can make things a bit easier with a bit of advice. Too many people buy clubs because they like the colour of the shafts or they have seen some golf pro on television ostensibly using a certain brand to win The Open. Just as standing in a church does not make you a Christian, buying the latest and most expensive driver does not mean you will be able to hit the damned thing.

A word of advice ... Learn to swing a club and hit a ball before you buy all of the kit. The golf swing is totally counter-intuitive. The more you try to hit the ball left, the further it will go to the right. Try to hit the cover off the ball and it will go ten feet and in the wrong direction. Working out in gymnasiums and developing bulging biceps with make your swing akin to a drunk using a sledgehammer to drive a nail ... and no amount of fancy equipment will make you hit the ball. The key is in the swing, not the equipment.

That being said, once a reasonable level of competence in striking the ball has been achieved, then modern clubs can certainly be helpful. (So will a prescription for Valium, which should be taken on the first tee.) The finest equipment will not keep all but the finest golfers from tensing every muscle in the upper body and holding in a full lungful of air, which immediately makes normally flexible muscles lock up like rusted hinges. The intended graceful swing then becomes something resembling a badly executed karate chop.

Nonetheless, technology has moved on, much as it has in tennis, squash, skiing, etc. If you really want to make a fool of yourself, try to hit a drive with an old club with a small persimmon head and a steel shaft. Your contact with the ball has to be perfect and the strike zone on the club head is tiny compared to modern clubs. They now design clubs with forgiveness and efficiency in mind. Thanks be to the normally merciless gods of golf for this small favour.

The clubs, which are often referred to as 'Woods', were designed to achieve distance off the tees and fairways. They are now made not of wood, but of metal and space age materials presumably to be used for intergalactic research missions. The aerodynamics of some drivers are now actually overseen by NASA, which makes many of us fear for the future of interplanetary travel. Head covers for woods used to be knitted to allow wet clubs to breathe and dry without warping. The new metal and plastic jobs are rustproof and can be housed in anything from fancy, over-sized head covers to freezer bags; they are indestructible.

Clubs can also be purchased in every shape and size imaginable. You can buy irons that look and behave like woods, 'hybrids', which are a cunning mixture supposedly between irons and woods, and irons with every type of head imaginable. A word to the wise ... so-called 'bladed' irons can only be hit properly by professionals and the rare breed with single digit handicaps. They give one a greater ability to control the flight of the ball for those that can hit them. For the rest of us, they are absolutely useless and should not even be considered.

To repeat, advice and counsel should be sought. Purchasing a set of golf clubs without it could be likened in its wisdom to removing your own appendix without instructions or anaesthesia. Something of an exaggeration perhaps, but the point is hopefully made.

CHAPTER THREE

An Introduction to Golf Courses ... And Their Codes of Conduct

Golfers exhibit enormous imagination in how they think they should behave and be attired to swing a stick at a ball. There are also codes of conduct depending on the type of golf course being played, and these codes can be both enforced or simply expected to be known and understood. Many have their basis in common sense ... some definitely do not. Attention should be paid to this section to avoid making a total ass of oneself in very short order.

What the novice to the game should know before playing any course is precisely how the club in question operates. What is the dress code, is there a handicap requirement, how much are the green fees, are there buggies available, etc.? There is no greater embarrassment than appearing for your round of golf and not being allowed to play. A couple of minutes on the telephonic communicator or a visit to the website will lay it all out.

There is one cardinal rule in golf ... *every golfer is expected to pay his own green fees*. Full stop. Exclamation mark. Unless the host very specifically says otherwise, always pay your own way. Gambling debts and green fees take priority over any other form of obligation!

Conduct on all golf courses should universally include a variety of common sense rules. Do not talk while someone is trying desperately to concentrate on hitting the ball and keep noise to a minimum, do not throw beer cans, food wrappers, etc. on the course.

There is little worse than trying to putt while some braying lout is laughing or yelling on the adjacent hole. Finally, try to limit bodily functions to designated facilities or places well-hidden in the shrubbery; deep bunkers and the back of *tee* boxes are not appropriate.

Keep noise to a minimum.

The low-end public course ... less than salubrious, to say the least.

CHAPTER FOUR

Low-End Public Golf Courses

These less than elegant venues provide an extraordinary insight into a sport which has been altered to include the widest possible slice of society as whole.

The least demanding golfing environment is the low-end public golf course, which can be seen in its purest form in the United States. Not a pretty sight!

These courses generally outlaw nudity, but virtually any body covering can be employed for the player to make it onto the course. String vests and T-shirts emblazoned with beer emblems or mindless slogans are extremely popular. Trousers or shorts are allowed in any form. Most popular seem to be the ubiquitous 'cargo shorts' which come in dung-hued shades and are covered with pockets to carry golf tees, bottle openers, knives, drugs and pistols. Socks are not required and the most popular golf shoe is the multicoloured trainer with thick soles and reflective bits. Headwear is invariably a baseball cap with the name of a football or baseball team emblazoned over the brim, often worn backwards for some unfathomable reason. All in all, a most unappealing sight.

Women can be seen in very short shorts or spandex with rolls of lard and pendulous breasts on full display. Men also seem to enjoy displaying their more repellant bits and pieces to the world using the sport as an excuse ... the more grotesque, the better ... or so it would seem. American golf courses lend themselves to this total lack of taste. They also insist on the use of buggies which means that overweight golfers do not have to take more than a few steps during a full round of eighteen holes.

It should be noted that trolleys of any type are prohibited on almost all courses of all types in the United States for reasons best known to themselves ... the principal motivation most probably being greed ... trolleys move more slowly than buggies. Buggies are required on public courses in the US as these are strictly commercial operations and they speed up play. The idea is to get as many unattractive people as possible packed on the course at any one time. Buggies also allow their inhabitants to carry six packs of chilled beer, cold pizza, sandwiches and other comestibles with them. There are also food carts which circulate constantly on such courses selling hot food, more cold beer, soft drinks, etc. Beer and cheeseburgers abound at every turn.

Buggies also allow their inhabitants to carry six packs of chilled beer and whatever else they might want to bring along as a playing companion.

There are usually giant trash bins to accommodate the rubbish, which in southern climes then attract packs of raccoons and other scavengers. They dine sumptuously on the leftovers and anything else left behind. On some courses the raccoons will actually jump into the buggies while you are playing a shot to steal your food, and alligators will approach golfers, as some idiots think it is amusing to feed them. Enormous venomous black water snakes also abound in the South, and an extraordinary variety of poisonous reptiles can be easily trodden on throughout the United States ... and I am not referring to the players! At times the wildlife can be the most challenging part of the American golfing experience.

The British and European versions of public courses are infinitely more civilised. There are dress codes, albeit often not rigidly enforced. There generally are buggies on offer, but many people use trolleys, both manual pull-trolleys and the electric jobs. The electric varieties come in various forms and the prices can vary from simply expensive to absurdly expensive, depending on the options chosen. There are varieties that fold up into themselves to save space but the unfolding and folding processes require an engineering degree from a good university. Errors can also cause involuntary amputation of cherished fingers. One can opt for lithium batteries, umbrella racks, course trackers, phone chargers, drinks holders, etc. so that the simple trolley resembles a badly assembled gypsy caravan.

CHAPTER FIVE

High-End Public Golf Courses

I would include in this group many of the better known courses in the United States and most courses in the United Kingdom and Europe. The green fees are higher, and certain dress restrictions are normally in place on both sides of the Atlantic. Short trousers are certainly discouraged in the UK, but still seem to emerge when the temperature rises above 25 degrees Centigrade. However, they are normally presentable in design and application.

In the USA things can be a bit different, as they increasingly feel that discriminating against inappropriate clothing is not politically correct. Also some courses are much more interested in getting as many people on the course as possible, regardless of whether they look as though they had dressed in a darkened basement while taking crack cocaine.

However, golfing on a decent course normally requires proper dress. Golf shoes, not trainers. Trousers. Shorts if necessary, but to just above the knee. For the ladies, trousers or skirts, and the skirts to be just above the knee ... otherwise when Madame is bending over to tee up a ball or collect it from the hole, her bits will be on display. This can lead to untoward behaviour by her playing companions in mixed foursomes, which will delay play and may lead to inconvenient lawsuits. Most embarrassing for all concerned.

Golfing on a decent course normally requires proper dress . . .

Coloured trousers and bright shorts are increasingly seen and are permissible. It is still a good idea to use a mirror when getting dressed, however. The custom of brightly coloured golf trousers began in America, the theory being that the golfer could be seen and it might discourage those playing behind you from firing golf balls in your direction. It does work. The British custom of playing in shades of brown and dark green is fine for deer stalking, but damned stupid on a golf course. A golf ball travelling at speed is to be avoided. The reasoning should be obvious to all but the most dimwitted of golfers.

CHAPTER SIX

Semi-Private Golf Courses

These exist more in the UK than in other countries. They have members who pay healthy annual dues and they play as often and whenever they wish. The public can also play, but they pay green fees for each round. These courses are normally well run and dress codes are thankfully enforced. Also, most of these courses are difficult enough and the terrain is testing enough to discourage the terminally fat and the totally inept. The risk of coronary occlusions and/or losing three balls per hole is a natural filtration system.

The vast majority of courses in the UK are available to members and the public alike, and this includes most of the finest golf courses in the world. Depending on the quality and fame of the course in question, the green fees for non-members can seem extremely high. However, if the highest fees in the UK are compared to the green fees charged in the rest of the world, golfing in the UK is still less expensive by a considerable margin. And there are extremely good, challenging and well-maintained courses all over the UK that are open to the public and very reasonably priced. No whingeing about green fees is allowed from the British golfing contingent.

As the members really run these clubs, they are interested in maintaining standards of both play and decorum. The quality of the course, the hiring and firing of green keepers, professionals and general staff are handled by a members' committee. Obviously the members want to make the club as attractive as possible in all respects to attract as many members as possible to offset the operating expenses. Expenses are also reduced by green fees from the public who, in turn, will also be attracted by a well run operation in a well maintained setting.

A player is sometimes seen on these courses in brightly checked trousers and a striped shirt, but thankfully such sights are increasingly a rarity, at least in the UK. There are two or three individuals on the professional tour that have lent their names to truly hideous clothing, but thankfully most people do have some sense of propriety and prefer not to be seen looking like they had dressed for a celebration of Halloween.

One final note ... the upper echelons of semi-private courses have one huge advantage ... caddies. They are a unique and marvellous breed. Playing the dreaded game accompanied by someone who normally has a single-digit handicap, can advise on all types of golf shots, and can see where the ball goes in deep fog, hail or snow is a real pleasure. Without a caddy on a proper links course one can easily lose a ball per hole ... the rough is knee deep in places, ankle deep in others, and swallows golf balls like a child eating Smarties.

Also, let's not forget that it is marvellous to have someone else carry the bag. Pulling trolleys, walking bent over like an elderly grave digger behind electric trolleys, or bouncing along in buggies are all guaranteed to accelerate spinal disintegration ... so caddies are a true luxury ... and should be treated as such!

Caddies are a true luxury, not beasts of burden.

A good caddy will also normally have a very dry sense of humour which will emerge, if allowed. Some rather stupid golfers look upon caddies as beasts of burden and little else, thereby missing their true value as companions and instructors. Caddies add to the game hugely. Their knowledge of the game is boundless. They also have rude and very non-PC nicknames for all types of bad shots ("Son-in-law", "Mexican", "Romanoff", etc.) and an endless stream of anecdotes which add to the jollity of the game. The odd wager also adds another dimension and caddies have been known to join in with a bit of side-betting as well. All in good fun.

The finest caddies in the world are found in Scotland. Most play to very low handicaps and are accustomed to playing golf in the most appalling conditions imaginable while maintaining their sense of humour. The good ones are great company on the course. The gentlemen pictured opposite, Duncan and Alan, are typical examples and they can be found plying their trade at Muirfield or Gullane in East Lothian.

Alan and Duncan, who will hopefully continue to be our friends long after our golfing days have ended.

The Membership Committee in operation.

CHAPTER SEVEN

Totally Private (Members Only) Golf Courses

There are relatively few of these rather rarified golf clubs which are totally private. To play as a non-member, one must be invited and accompanied by a member. They are owned by the members. A new member pays an initiation fee to become a member, and an annual charge is paid thereafter which usually represents a percentage share of the annual operating costs of the club. The membership elects a board of directors or a management committee to be in charge of running the club and they are responsible to the members. Members must be invited to be members, and their candidacy is submitted to a membership committee which can deny their admission for whatever reason they see fit. All extremely logical, as the members own the club. A private club is not a public facility. It is not a bus station.

One often hears the politically correct and excessively liberal mob bleating about such institutions being stuffy, discriminatory, old-fashioned, intrinsically nasty and exclusionary. The answer is very simple. Such clubs are on private land which is owned by the members of the club. The land has been made into a golf course. As it is private land, the owners can choose to have it be pastureland for cows, install a pig farm, or make it into a sporting facility. It is private, just as one's home is private ... and just as with one's home, the owner can choose to invite anyone he wants into his home and keep everyone else the hell out. A very simple concept.

Private clubs are operated with the idea that the members are like-minded souls who will actually want to spend time together, a home away from home, if you will. No one forces anyone to be a member of a private club, and if someone takes offence at their existence, they can form their own club! Anyone taking offence should have a peek at their nearest dictionary and check the definitions of 'private' and 'public'.

There are many more truly private golf clubs in the United States than there are in the UK and Europe, which may be due to the fact that land was relatively inexpensive and plentiful in the USA when most of these clubs were formed. The funding was private in most cases, i.e., a group of people put up their own money to buy the land, form the club, build the golf course and clubhouse, and then invited friends and family to be members.

In America golf was originally an elitist sport, available mainly at private clubs. This has now changed drastically and there is a plethora of golf courses available to everyone, almost everywhere in the country. The popularity of the sport has expanded exponentially, as it has in the UK. However, the totally private clubs still exist on both sides of the Pond.

So much for philosophy. The realities of the private clubs vary from the interesting to the amusing. In the UK there are relatively few truly private clubs. However, the top truly private courses date back generations and many of the customs of these somewhat anachronistic institutions have remained since the clubs were founded.

For example, one such club in England allows totally unleashed dogs on the course and the club has lady members ... the ladies are allowed in the bar and the dogs are not. Another very old club nearby allows dogs in the bar but not ladies.

Other English courses will allow short trousers to the knee, but they must only be worn with knee length socks. Needless to say, this rule catches many guests unawares and the pro shops sell rather a lot of knee socks! Another course allows women to play on the course (when invited) but there are no changing facilities for them and no ladies' tees. Almost all such clubs insist that jackets and ties be worn when men are dining other than in the bar area, and many players shower and bring a change of clothes to wear in the dining room. All very civilised. People of a certain age should stay well covered up in public anyway.

Such club rules, on both sides of the Atlantic, archaic though they may be, were all put in place in a different era. However, they will quite rightly remain in effect until the members of the private clubs involved decide to change them. If the left-wing contingent finds it all irritating, they are free to establish their own clubs where they give membership to whoever they wish. The men can wear skirts, the ladies can play naked, and live chickens can be kept in the bar area.

CHAPTER EIGHT

Golf Lessons

There is an old adage that says, 'An attorney who defends himself has a fool for a client.' In a similar vein, anyone who thinks they can teach themselves how to swing a golf club has a fool for a pupil.

A proper golf swing has a wide variety of component parts and could be likened to a fine mechanical watch ... if one small piece is missing or malfunctions the whole thing is up the spout! If the various parts all work together properly, the result is a good ball strike. If not, as was said by a well known golf commentator, 'It's like watching a drunk chasing a balloon near the edge of a cliff.' And God alone knows where the ball can end up.

Golf instructors are thick on the ground and each one has his own approach to teaching the basics. Some will start by having the pupils try to hit the ball with their eyes closed. This increases awareness of balance and a smooth swing. All true, but it makes the pupil feel like a complete twit doing it. Others will have you swing the club like a baseball bat and then do the same while bent at the waist. Or imitate throwing a bucket of water at the target ... at times it is very tempting to throw a bucket of water on the golf pro after half an hour of sheer frustration ...

The upshot is that instruction is absolutely vital. Otherwise you simply do what is comfortable and seems to be a natural swing. This will always, without any question, be the absolute reverse of what should be done, and then you will have to unlearn everything before starting all over again. It is a bit like building an atom bomb . . . you may as well learn to do it the right way from the outset.

Find a golf pro that suits your mentality and that has a simplistic approach. Some pros are too technical and the brain cannot absorb endless little adjustments, let alone try to think of them when addressing the ball. Start with one or two basics, do them properly until they become automatic, and then proceed to the next stage. The worst and most disheartening thing possible is to start by trying to hit with a driver. The longer the club, the more it will accentuate defects in the golf swing. Start with a relatively short club and work up. Otherwise there will be a lot of wailing, gnashing of teeth, and very bad language, regardless of sexual orientation or upbringing.

Also, seek out a professional who has been properly trained. You would not go to a surgeon without checking his credentials unless you are a complete moron. The same applies to golf pros. Cheap may be cheerful, but the damage can take years to undo. Good golf pros, like good doctors and lawyers, are not inexpensive. One good lesson is definitely worth ten bad ones. You get what you pay for in life, and you have taken up a sport which will wreak serious damage to your bank account anyway.

Some pros are too technical and the brain cannot absorb endless little adjustments.

If you find a good pro that suits you, stay with them and take their advice. They now have the technology to analyse your swing down to the minutest detail, and there can be no one better to advise on clubs, shafts, club length, etc. Clubs can be precisely adapted to suit you ... or a one-armed gorilla with a limp, for that matter.

One size does not fit all. Buying golf equipment is exactly like buying shoes or a pair of trousers ... buy them to fit. All decent brands of club have an endless choice of club heads, shafts, etc. and the mysteries can only be unravelled by a professional. Find a good one. Word of mouth is a good starting point. Ask golfing friends who they use and why. Then if it all ends up being a disaster, at least you have someone to blame.

CHAPTER NINE

The

Novice Golfer

The definition of a novice is basically a beginner or a learner ... or in the case of a religious order, an initiate. This extraordinary game is much more than a mere religion ... it can quickly become an obsession both in practice and in the ceremony that surrounds it. Thus perhaps the term 'initiate' would be more appropriate for those donning the mantle of madness referred to as Golf.

The first layer of initiates is the young, fresh-faced children who are often thrust on to a golf range by their parents before their joints have even formed properly. Cartilage is still in its most formative stages and the golf-mad parent has the poor dribbler out there slashing away at golf balls for hours. 'Look at his fluid swing ... what flexibility', will often be heard. Yes, the child is flexible because his connective tissue has not formed sufficiently to restrict his or her movements. The golf swing puts the human body into contortions normally reserved for carnival performers. Orthopaedic surgeons can often be seen with a sly and greedy gleam in their eye while watching children practice golf. This is not odd behaviour on their part ... it is financial planning.

The golf swing puts the human body into contortions normally reserved for carnival performers.

If properly coached, a child can be introduced to the wonders of the game without incurring a crippling physical disability. They will then hopefully carry their training on into their lives and derive huge pleasure from being regaled as a 'natural golfer' by those less fortunate souls who spent their childhood learning lesser disciplines . . . such as mathematics, spelling, etc.

Like any sport learned at an early age, the golf swing and course etiquette will remain ingrained for life. This is, in fact, a huge advantage, as golf unquestionably becomes the most desirable of sports as age limits mobility and reflexes. A few torn ligaments, hip and/ or knee replacements and frozen shoulders later, golf looms large on the horizon as the only way to get some exercise and fresh air for those not satisfied with beer and computer games. Learning as a young dribbler pays dividends when one is an old dribbler.

Learning golf is, for children, a relative doddle. A good professional will teach them the basics, supervise them on a sporadic basis, and a golfer is born. However, none of the above applies past the onset of adolescence. This may be due to the lack of concentration displayed by most teenagers, but also for some reason the onset of raging hormones brings tension and aggression to physical movement. This probably dates back to when pubescent children were expected to earn their keep by chasing down Mastodons, but it is true. Teaching a relatively sedate and passive game like golf to a teenager is comparable to teaching chess to a hungry monkey. It can be done, but with some difficulty.

If a dedicated parent can impose their will on both the child and the beleaguered golf professional to persevere, a golfer will emerge. The golf swing is basically a series of unnatural movements strung together, and practice over an extended period is needed so that this athletic symphony can be ingrained in the memory. If a child can be induced through bribery or threat of bodily injury to make a serious and ongoing effort to learn the game, it can be a great source of pleasure for all concerned in later years. Parents should keep this in mind when dragging a sullen and unwilling teenager to the golf course when it would rather be playing computer games in a darkened basement with its monosyllabic and unattractive peers.

The third basic of type of golfing novice encompasses those who did not have the good fortune to learn the game in their youth. This means anyone who picks up a club for the first time in their twenties onward. Obviously learning any sport becomes more difficult as the decades pass, but learning new and unnatural movements as an adult is both challenging and unsightly. If you give any normal adult a stick and then ask them to hit a small object with it, the result will not in any way resemble a golf swing.

A perfect example of the perversity of golf is the fact that there are three possible ways to hold a golf club . . . the most comfortable is the least desirable. Golf techniques have been devised over the years by thousands of people trying desperately to consistently hit the ball where they would like it to go. Thus far the 'consistent' part continues to be absent from the formula. Robotics may be the only solution . . .

Adulthood brings with it the ability to reason and to see things from various perspectives. Such tendencies must be totally ignored in golf. If someone is trying to hit out at an attacking snake, they would begin the movement with the dominant hand. In golf the dominant hip starts the movement, then the shoulder and the hands lag behind. If the ball were a venomous snake, death would be a certainty. The golf swing must be learned by rote, not by logically trying to sequence movements to hit the ball. Any semblance of rational thought would immediately dictate taking up another pastime.

Aside from the limitations on learning imposed by age, the sheer ability to move decreases astronomically with each birthday. As the movements required in golf can be a bit 'forced' to say the least, the strain on stiff muscles, calcified ligaments and increasingly arthritic joints can bring tears of joy to the eyes of any chiropractor. Stand quietly beside any practice tee and one can hear the gentle squeaking of prolapsing discs. The correct 'follow through' of a good golf swing has crippled many an exceptional athlete, let alone the spinal havoc that can be wreaked on a slightly overstuffed middle-aged sofa dweller.

All of the above notwithstanding, golf is the most challenging, addictive and obsessive game ever devised. Marriages crumble, family units disintegrate, overdrafts spiral ... all sacrificed to the grinning gods of golf. Step this way into the bottomless pit of physical and psychological frustration which somehow attracts people like no other sport. When is the last time you saw a tennis player practising his backhand in the drawing room or a skier poised on his skis in the bedroom? Golfers regularly practise putts in the office, try to chip over the sofa into a wastebasket, and hit plastic balls into a net on the lawn.

On a very rare basis the novice will hit a good shot, and that is enough to bring him or her back. One decent shot in twenty, or thirty, or fifty will be enough to make you know you can do it ... and that is the vision of the Holy Grail that begins the obsession. Welcome to the world of golf ...

CHAPTER TEN

The Experienced Golfer

The term 'experience' when applied to golf really refers to time and money spent . . . In most cases, an experienced golfer will have achieved some level of competence at this evil game. That can mean anything from being able to hit the ball in some approximation of the right direction to being able to actually play the game to a reasonable standard. There are, admittedly, some fortunate souls who can be very irritating by playing the game extremely well. They carry with them an air of undeniable superiority and should be charged a surtax of at least ten per cent on all golf related bills to pay for lessons for the rest of us.

Playing the game over a period of time generally means that one is a member of at least one golf club, understands the etiquette of the game and behaves reasonably well while playing. Loud screams of frustration and excessively bad language have disappeared, and have been replaced by mumbling, occasional whimpering and body movements which are meant to actually change the flight of the golf ball. Basic physics will tell you that extreme cocking of the head and contorting the lower body will not affect moving objects. Such movements can, however, change the position of a lumbar disc, which in turn changes the bank balance of the local chiropractor or physiotherapist.

Chiropractors, by the way, love golfers over the age of forty. Without golfers, this arcane art of spinal manipulation would have gone the way of medicinal leeching. Chiropractors on the whole seem to be judged about the same way as a fireworks display ... they are paid for the noise. If they can evoke a terrifying cracking sound from the spinal area, it is a sign of success.

A good physiotherapist, on the other hand, is a gift from the gods. They are less extreme but more effective. They work on the muscles, and can make an enourmous difference ... as in playing vs. not playing.

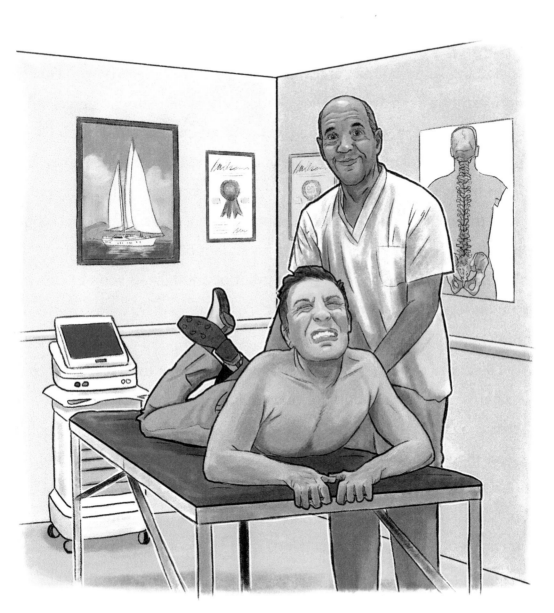

A dedicated and brilliant physiotherapist, like our dear friend Rogerio, can be a true-lifesaver.

The totally unnatural contortions required to play golf become even more extreme as the novice tries desperately to emulate the perceived ideal swing, all the while compensating for an endless array of bodily malfunctions which seem to increase exponentially with age. Hence one of the many golf related pastimes is spending vast sums of folding on the elimination of pain. Massage, manipulation, exercise teachers, yoga, shiatsu, healing hands, and an endless stream of legal and illegal pharmaceuticals are all tried at one point or another. As soon as one pain lessens, another emerges.

The experienced golfer will also always be trying to improve his or her game. Hit the drive further, putt straighter, chip with backspin, achieve a consistent draw as opposed to a screaming hook, stop hitting across the ball so it bleeds off like a Russian prince, etc. This endless quest involves burning cash at an appalling rate ... Technology moves on, but not at the rate often claimed by equipment manufacturers. However, golf is a game which lends itself to constant 'tweaking'. If something is working well, a small change will make it work better, right? No further comment needed.

Have a look at the myriad players on the American and European Tours; every swing is different. Every pre-swing ritual is different. They all address the ball in a slightly different way. Some use long putters, others use putters so short that the players hands are at knee level ... again, the chiropractor's dream! They even grip the club differently, especially when putting. As a famed British golfer and commentator, once remarked over global television while watching one pro putt, 'The last time I saw a grip like that was in the Men's Room at Wentworth.'

Once a golfer feels that he or she has a reasonable grasp of the game is precisely when the fun really begins. This is the moment that every golf pro, club fitter and equipment outlet waits for. University educations, new cars, house extensions are all paid for by experienced golfers seeking a magic cure. Different shafts, new clubs, different balls, endless mechanical devices that hang from ones head, attach to the club, or lie in the ground are on offer and are greedily snapped up by an expanding audience. Also, as physical disabilities increase, so does the available gimmickry. In the case of golf, experience does not necessarily breed wisdom.

The committed golfer often makes enormous sacrifices for his sport ... employment and marriages fail as routine responsibilities pale in significance. Feeding the upturned mouths of children becomes secondary to the purchase of the latest cavity-backed irons. Anniversary and birthday gifts are overlooked and replaced by the purchase of a new driver or the latest hand-crafted putter. True commitment to the game is often characterised by blank staring at the dinner table, waking in the pre-dawn hours with an overwhelming desire to practise the takeaway move, and practising a new grip on a salad fork. Things can also get a bit beady when one's other half does not share and therefore understand the obsessive behaviour of dedicated golfers.

As yet, playing golf is not considered on its own to be grounds for divorce, but it certainly has often been used by unamused spouses to support a claim of 'mental cruelty'. Bottom-feeding divorce lawyers have been known to join golf clubs in their unceasing search for potential clients. It is difficult for many to comprehend that practising one's putting can lead to wintry evenings spent sleeping on the street with a golf bag clutched to the breast for companionship.

CHAPTER ELEVEN

Male vs. Female Golfers

The Male Contingent:

The male animal sees everything through a faint mist of testosterone. Even a rather reserved and slow-paced sport like golf brings out the innate aggression that lies just below the surface of all men. No matter how much concentration is spent on a smooth, relaxed swing, as soon as the club begins its downward arc the red mist descends. The entire upper torso, shoulders, arms and hands tense up as though the golfer was trying to kill an alligator with a walking stick. 'Just this once I will hit the cover off the damned ball and it will go straight.' Best of British luck, as they say . . .

Female golfer: *Distance is achieved through good timing, not brute strength.*

Male golfer: *No matter how much concentration is spent on a smooth, relaxed swing, as soon as the club begins its downward arc the red mist descends.*

Unless the game is learned at a very early age, the principal obstacle that must be overcome by men is aggression, which breeds rigidity. A relaxed, flowing swing is the ideal and the greatest distance, control and pleasure will result … or so we are told by an endless stream of professionals. Men are not naturally graceful. The millennia have genetically ingrained a chromosome which controls physical movement in the male animal. Since the beginning of time, men being graceful brought ridicule from their peers, and being relaxed brought death.

Therefore, oddly enough, a middle-aged man is often better taught by a female professional. Unless the lady is built like a discus thrower, she will concentrate on the swing path and rhythm rather than trying to hit the cover off the ball. No matter how hard men try, they will always teach an aggressive swing, which is often not helpful … and incessant practice of aggressive body movements almost invariably leads to (a) hours spent in physiotherapy, (b) a foul disposition and (c) a massive ingestion of pain-killers.

Men are also deeply conscious of status. They do not like to admit this, but it is true. Status can be a matter of simply playing the game well. However, most golfers do not play the game well enough to derive any status from their athletic competence. Only a lucky few can rely on having a relatively low handicap. Others gain status through winning competitions by maintaining a high handicap, which in turn wins the dislike of their peers and earns them the reputation of being a 'bandit'. In point of fact, people who try to manipulate their handicaps are idiots; the only people they are cheating are themselves.

Men also are keen on their 'toys', which can cover a broad spectrum ranging from yachts to key chains. So ... golf equipment becomes a status symbol. The latest clubs, a spiffy golf bag, golf shoes, the latest shirts being worn by one's favourite professional golfer, etc., ad infinitum. But, herein lies the rub, as they say ...

As the choice of golf courses and golfing venues improves, the phenomenon of 'reverse chic' kicks in. It definitely becomes admired to use the oldest clubs possible (preferably well worn and slightly rusted), a shabby old golf bag, slightly baggy and well worn chinos, an old faded golf shirt, or even a collared shirt with the sleeves rolled up, and a hat that looks like it had been chewed by a camel. This final look is most effective when it is accompanied on the course by two Labradors and a scruffy terrier.

Thus, sartorial status for the male golfer can be graphed very easily in the monetary sense. The golfing career begins with low expenditure and the overall cash outlay gradually increases. It moves from t-shirts, cargo shorts and trainers up to the latest kit, which changes every year. Then as a golfer ages a bit and becomes more sophisticated, shabby becomes better and the expenditure curve diminishes to nearly zero. The graph looks roughly like a drawing of Mount Kilimanjaro. Wives tend to be rather cranky as the top of the mountain is being reached. By the time it tapers off, they have either ceased caring or a divorce has occurred.

The Female Contingent:

On the other hand, the female golfing contingent has its own characteristics, many of which will be vociferously denied by the ladies. They do undeniably bring grace and rhythm to the game. Distance is achieved through good timing, not brute strength. 'Swat and Swear' often summarises the male game, but the ladies have more finesse. Perhaps yoga classes and stretching exercises come to the fore as opposed to bicep curls and deep squats. Whatever the reason, it is definitely ballet vs. bulldozers.

However, in general women are infinitely more serious and precise than men in their adherence to and interpretation of the rules of golf. Millimetres matter hugely in ball placement. Bunker shots are viewed through narrowed eyes, ever seeking grounds for a one stroke penalty. Lengths of twine are carried to string between Out of Bounds markers. Terrifying stuff!

Scoring is of major importance and precision is required. Men often give six-foot putts and concede holes in order to get to the bar more quickly. The ladies will examine putts from all angles, concessions are rare, and competition is fierce. This is all very intimidating to those who look at golf as an excuse for a long walk in the countryside with like-minded souls.

A word of warning to both sexes ... beware the Ladies' Golf Committee in any golf club. They are akin to the Comintern in the days when the Kremlin was operating at full bore during the Cold War. In contrast, the men's committees generally meet in the bar over multiple refreshing beverages with bowls of chips. Decisions of any consequence are rare.

The ladies, on the other hand, prefer tea and efficiency. Raucous laughter, bad language and off-colour sexist jokes do not abound. Designated roles within the ladies' committee structure are fulfilled with strict adherence to decorum. Men have been known to linger tenuously in the parking lot or go home to mow the lawn when the ladies' committees are in full swing.

Ladies are also infinitely more conscious of the dress codes and will impose them vigorously. Fashion and colours play a major role, as do hair styles, hats and shoe styles. This compares favourably to the rumpled trousers and shirts stretched over expanding stomachs favoured on the men's tees. Stained and wrinkled clothing are frowned upon by the ladies and largely accepted by the men. It is a different world, and ne'er the twain shall meet . . .

The author on a bad day.

CHAPTER TWELVE

When to give up the Game

Time moves on, regardless of the efforts of the pharmaceutical companies and plastic surgeons to delay its effects. The previously young and supple gives way to the slow and ponderous. The evolution of the golfer as a physical specimen is not a pretty sight to behold, nor is the golf swing which deteriorates at roughly the same rate. Basically once a man or a woman is unable to stand upright, look down and see their feet, a decent golf swing becomes less of a reality. As the effects of arthritis, clinical obesity and loss of mental acuity take hold, golf courses also thankfully become less appealing. Life does have its compensations . . .

Basically any sport should be abandoned when it becomes less than amusing. Golf is, after all, a game. Nothing more, nothing less. Some may make a living doing it, but it is a game for most players. When it stops being fun, or the pain exceeds the pleasure, it is perhaps time to move on.

If an experienced player has spent the last few years hitting long, straight shots and now is hitting half the distance and into the bushes with no improvement in sight, then it is time to think of other diversions. Bridge, online gambling, pole dancing clubs ... the possibilities both legal and illegal are endless. One does not want to continue playing to the point that every shot brings forth groans of disappointment or pain, or both.

*Bridge, online gambling, pole dancing clubs..... the possibilities
both legal and illegal are endless.*

The abandonment process is gradual. We begin playing a bit less ...
nine holes, not eighteen ... twice a week, not five times ... no more
club matches. The bar, a pint and some chips with burnt sausages are
now the best part of the game. The garden and the mowing may take
on new appeal. The children have flown and one is suddenly left staring
at one's significant other, which in this day and age may consist of
almost anything, male or female or a mixture of both, animal or human
... but whatever it is, it will have aged while one has been
concentrating on golf. This revelation may come as a bit of a shock and
time to adjust might be spent in the garden shed with a bottle of gin.

A replacement for the delights of golf must be found but this must be
left to the individual devices of each ex-golfer. There is no social
algorithm which will compute everyone's situation and spit out a
solution. Each to their own, but the absence of the golfing obsession
will be a real life-changer. Therefore do not give it up until it is
absolutely unbearable to continue. And if you do stop playing, don't tell
anyone at home! Otherwise management will insist on your presence at
the home front for gutter cleaning and wood splitting.

CHAPTER THIRTEEN

The Future ...
The PCGC

Both the world and the game of golf are changing at a truly astonishing rate. The popularity of sport in general and golf in particular is skyrocketing; witness the number of television and satellite channels dedicated solely to golf. Every tournament is covered, whether held in lofty mountains, desert sands, or dismal hamlets in the bowels of America. There are crowds of screaming fans surrounding every hole, becoming louder, more profane and more badly behaved every year. Soon the professional players will have to have their eardrums deadened by injection before teeing off.

Geographic and social mobility are now taken for granted, and governmental regulations have grown out of all proportion. All of these factors combined with an obsession with political correctness in the two major homes of golf, the United Kingdom and the United States, and the stage is set for major changes in the game in the coming decades.

As the popularity of the game continues to expand, there will be increasing social pressure to make the sport freely available to everyone. The golf courses that already exist will probably remain largely unchanged, but new courses could be built, funded by the government, aka, the taxpayer. These courses would be tightly regulated and supervised by the politically correct bureaucrats who even now codify how we must all think and act. These would be known as Politically Correct Golf Courses, or PCGCs.

. . . there will be a representative of the People's Sport Police at each PCGC, dressed in protective helmets, eye protectors and reflective suits.

On these open access PCGC courses, free to all, there would be no men's or women's tees ... that would be sexist and discriminatory. There would be no tees for over seventies ... that would be ageist and discriminatory. There would be no white, blue or red tees, as that would be discriminatory, nationalistic and would deeply offend the delicate egos of multicultural players. There would be no dress or behavioural codes, as that might discriminate against the less educated or less disciplined members of this wondrous future society.

Of course there would have to be a representative of the People's Sport Police at each PCGC, dressed in protective helmets, eye protectors and high visibility outfits. They would, clip boards clutched in hand, evaluate players' abilities in a sympathetic and non-offensive manner. Each player would then be offered one of many tees to play from. The tee boxes could all be named after flowers, so there would be no suggestion of numerical or sexual ranking, which again would be extremely damaging to the psyches of the players. Of course, any differentiation between players based on religion, physical condition, sexual orientation or ability in the PCGCs would be strictly prohibited.

The imagination can run totally amok with the endless possibilities. There could be counselling and classes for those participating in Trans-Golf, Obeso-Golf and Altzo-Golf. Special equipment would be available to offer assistance when necessary. The marvels of modern surgery might make the addition of extra limbs possible when needed for those whose body weight can not be carried by only two legs. Hence the increasingly obese population would not be excluded from the magic of Golf. Trousers with additional legs could then be on offer in the PCGC golf shops in a variety of bright colours, as would specialised clothing to make gender identification totally impossible.

In addition, all tracking devices to find wanderers, mobility equipment and other specialised golfing items purchased by PCGC members would obviously be paid for by the National Health Service in the UK or ObamaCare in the USA. Golf could become the ultimate example of multi-cultural, socialised sport ... a beacon ... Karl Marx in plaid shorts! Don't laugh, it could happen.

The wondrous game of Golf has come a long way since its humble beginnings in the Scottish countryside, but there seems to be no limit in sight to the absurdities that the future could hold in store. May we all keep our senses of humour and our health ... we will definitely need both! And now, off to the bar ...

AUTHORS NOTE

Golf is a cruel game, but a game nonetheless. All of the elements of nature plus the idiosyncracies of your own body will constantly conspire against you. In the face of such challenges, the only reply is laughter and the shaken fist of good humour.

CCH

A portion of the proceeds from the sale of this book will go to the
Lt Dougie Dalzell MC Memorial Trust (DDMT) formed after the tragic death
of Dougie Dalzell on his 27th birthday in Helmand, Afghanistan.

Dougie had an inherent concern for the welfare of his men. This is the
founding principle upon which the Trust, which is also a Charity, was built.
DDMT prides itself on being able to react flexibly to requirements of
beneficiaries that may have fallen through the gaps of traditional and
larger charitable organisations.

More details can be found at www.ddmt.co.uk or email info@ddmt.co.uk

Lt Dougie Dalzell MC

The local wildlife always has its own role in the game.

Lightning Source UK Ltd.
Milton Keynes UK
UKOW07n0637210617
303748UK00005B/22/P